PALM BEACH COUNTY
LIBRARY SYSTEM
3650 Summit Boulevard
West Palm Beach, FL 33406-4198

Curious George®
Roller Coaster

Adaptation by Monica Perez
Based on the TV series teleplay
written by Lazar Saric

Houghton Mifflin Harcourt
Boston New York

For information about permission to reproduce selections from this book, write to trade.permissions@hmhco.com or to Permissions, Houghton Mifflin Harcourt Publishing Company, 3 Park Avenue, 19th Floor, New York, New York 10016.

Library of Congress Cataloging-in-Publication Data

Perez, Monica.
Curious George roller coaster / adaptation by Monica Perez.
  p. cm.
  "Based on the TV series teleplay written by Lazar Saric."
  ISBN-13: 978-0-618-80040-7 (pbk. : alk. paper)
  ISBN-10: 0-618-80040-9 (pbk. : alk. paper)
  I. Saric, Lazar. II. Curious George (Television program) III. Title.
  PZ7.P42583Cuw 2007
  [Fic]—dc22
  2006101438

Design by Joyce White

www.hmhco.com

Manufactured in China
SCP 18 17 16 15 14 13 12 11
4500798622

George woke his friend up early.
Today was a special day.
They were going to Zany Island!

George was curious about riding the
roller coaster.
It was called the Turbo Python 3000.

It looked scary and fun.

Betsy and Steve had ridden it nine times!

They invited George to ride with them.
But there was a problem.
George was too short.

The man at the gate said George needed
to be five candy strings tall to ride.
George was only four.

How could George grow one candy
string in a day?
Maybe he could eat leaves like a giraffe.
Giraffes were tall.

Yuck!

The leaves tasted bad.

George took a bite of his candy string.

Candy tasted better.

What else could
he do to grow?
George thought exercising might help.
He lifted a heavy bar.

Then George measured himself.
He was now four and a half
candy strings tall!

George wondered if stretching
would make him grow.
He tried it.
By this time George was very tired.
He nibbled on his candy some more.

George saw a mother and baby.
The mother told the baby that sleep
would help him grow.
So George took a nap too.

When he woke,
he measured again.
Hooray! He was finally five candy
strings tall.

But the sign said he was still too
short to ride.
How could that be?

"Have you been biting your candy strings, George?" the man with the yellow hat asked.

George nodded.

"When the candy strings were longer,
it took four to measure you," the man
explained.
"Now that the candy strings
are shorter, it takes more of them to
measure you—five.
But you did not grow."

George was so disappointed.
Captain Zany, the park owner, walked by.
When he heard about George's
problem, he smiled.
"Since monkeys don't grow very tall,
we have a special sign for them."

Was George tall enough now?
You bet he was!

HOW DOES IT MEASURE UP?

Measuring tools you will need:

Empty paper towel roll
Empty toilet paper roll
Large paper clip

Using each item in turn, measure the following distances. Fill in the chart with your measurements. Which distance was the largest? Did you get the same answer using all three methods of measurement?

	Paper Towel Roll	Toilet Paper Roll	Large Paper Clip
Length of your bed			
Height of the kitchen table			
Distance between your sofa and TV			

Delving deeper:

1. Which measuring tool was quickest to use?
2. Which measuring tool was most accurate (you did not have to estimate halves or "round up")?

Answers:

1. The paper towel roll would be quickest because it is the largest.

2. The paper clip would give the most accurate measurement. You would not have to "round up" much or at all. But it would be very hard to measure a very long distance with such a small instrument. The size of the object or the distance you measure can vary. This is why we use many different standards of measurement such as an inches, feet, yards, and miles.

Chart Your Height

Start with a very long sheet of butcher paper or cut open some paper grocery bags and tape them together. Take a ruler or yardstick and draw a line down the edge of the longest side of the paper. Mark off inches all the way up the line.

Decorate your chart with paints, markers, crayons, or stickers.

Before you hang the chart on a wall, measure two feet up from the ground and mark the wall lightly with pencil. Leave this space empty. Place your chart so that its bottom is at the two-foot mark.

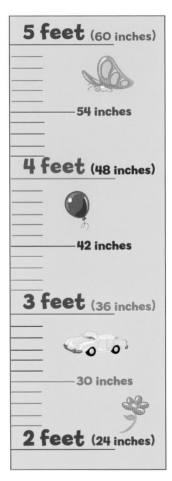

5 feet (60 inches)

54 inches

4 feet (48 inches)

42 inches

3 feet (36 inches)

30 inches

2 feet (24 inches)

Write "two feet" at the bottom of your chart and label every twelfth inch as three feet, four feet, five feet, etc.

Then stand against the chart and have a parent or friend mark your current height with pen or permanent ink on the chart. Label this line with the date and your age. Now when people ask, you can tell them exactly how tall you are!

Every six months, have someone mark your new height. You can probably use this chart for several years. When you are too tall for it, you can take it down, fold it up, and keep it as a record of how fast you grew.